The Borrowed Property Strategy

How anyone can generate an income from other people's properties, using Serviced Accommodation

Copyright

No part of this book may be reproduced or transmitted in any form or by any means, electronic or mechanical, including photocopying, recording or by any information storage and retrieval system, without written permission from the author.

Disclaimer

The information provided within this book is for general informational purposes only. While we try to keep the information up-to-date and correct, there are no representations or warranties, express or implied, about the completeness, accuracy, reliability, suitability or availability with respect to the information, products, services, or related graphics contained in this book for any purpose. Any use of this information is at your own risk.

Acknowledgements

I wish to dedicate this book to my parents, who have been my everlasting supporters throughout my turbulent journey as an entrepreneur, who have always supported me even through my crazy ideas and endeavours. I am eternally grateful for teaching me that I could accomplish anything and everything I set my heart to.

Finally, I would like to thank you for picking up this book and trusting me to shares my experiences, my insights, and my heart with you, so you can fulfil your property dreams and goals. I am grateful.

Contents

Why would a landlord give you their property for Rent to Serviced Accommodation?

> **- My secret sauce for deals**
> **- Dwayne (Client)**

Who uses Serviced Accommodation? (Customer Types & Quick customer analysis)

What types of properties work for Serviced Accommodation?

Protect the asset

Location Analysis

Listing your property

      Airbnb

      Booking.com

Photography

Live examples of our Serviced Accommodation properties

Where to find suitable Serviced Accommodation properties

Realistic Costs of starting a Rent to Rent Serviced Accommodation business

Casestudy #1 - Stay City
Casestudy #2 - Saco Apartments

Why Corporates and Companies choose Serviced Accommodation over hotels

Can I show you how and why smart property entrepreneurs are flooding into the Serviced Accommodation market?

Why should you start a Rent to Rent Serviced Accommodation business?

What your Serviced Accommodation should look like

Legals
    - Rules & Regulations

Quick Fire – Answering my most asked questions

Hi Tj, **What is the best way to get started?**

Hi Tj, **How do I make money from this strategy?**

Hi Tj, **I don't have the funds to get started!**

Hi Tj, **What types of properties can I rent for my Serviced Accommodation business?**

Hi Tj, **Should I self-managed or give the property to a Management company?**

Hi Tj, **How do I get my 1st property?**

Hi Tj, **How much should I spend on prepping the property/ refurbishment?**

Hi Tj, **Can I insure the property?**

Hi Tj, **I loved this book and I would love to go to the next step?**

Testimonials & Reviews

- Denzel
- Ashley
- Charlotte
- Nicole
- Kabir
- Leah
- Aliyah
- Pelegia
- Epi
- Rochael
- Joan
- Sabha
- Ezugo
- Morenike
- Khadija
- Funke

Educational Purposes

This book is a guide and should be used for educational purposes only.

I have taken careful steps to demonstrate how myself and my clients do things in our property business[es]. I am aware there are various ways to running a successful property business. This book, is based on our experiences, mistakes and insights.

This book should not be considered as legal or financial advice. Rules, laws, regulations change regularly. Please make yourself familiar with them.

Falling into property

Growing up in a council estate in London, surrounded by more council estates, overlooking a few posher council estates meant property was always on my mind, not because, I thought one day I would become a landlord or go on to own multiple properties, but simply because it seemed like we were trapped in a world of intensive property poverty and there was no opportunity to escape.

Growing up in a council felt like prison.

Although, I acknowledge I have never been to prison, but if you can imagine the feeling of been trapped, surrounded by run down government owned buildings and knowing deep within your heart, that you could not escape, not because you were forced to stay, but simply because no one ever escapes. No one ever breaks free. That certainly felt like prison to me.

Although as a child, I dreamt about property daily, property investing was the last thing on my mind.

I despised the *'establishment'*. As a young man, I assumed, that property was owned by the government rather than individual landlords. I grew to hate property, the local councils, the government and anyone associated with it.

Our council estate staircase would usually have drugs openly spew on the floor or if no drugs were found, we would be lucky to have urine in the staircase rather than the occasional dog or human excrement which would slowly permeate the entrance way. "The government doesn't care about us", I would lament, "otherwise they would not allow us to live like this."

I recalled visiting a school friend Tafik's house and seeing his beautiful, warm and cosy home. I was quick to note, that there was no damp or no faecal smell. I was confused, why would the government give him and his family such a beautiful house and us, a horrible, disgusting cramped flat.

I remember saying to his dad, "nice house, you guys are lucky they gave you this." His reply completely changed my life.

"Gave us? what do you mean Tj, we bought this!"…

I ran home, grinning like an excited child. I remember, my mum and dad we in the living room (which also doubled up as bedroom) as one of our room was mould infested.

"Mum, Dad, we are moving. I know how we can get out of this place. I know a secret". My mum's ears pricked up. "Go on," she indulged me.

"Are you actually listening? I positioned myself in front of the television, to ensure I had their full attention.

"Well, did you know that you could buy property. Did you know it was possible. The government doesn't own it all. Let's buy something near Nick's house". I rambled without taken a breath.

"Yes, of course we know you can buy", mum replied.

"So why are we living here, why don't we buy," I hit her again with a barrage of questions.

"Because we simply can't afford it", she replied.

I climbed back into my bunkbed and fell asleep.

How life changes eh. Between my mum and I, we now multiple properties, land, a commercial office building and a mechanic.

The reality is that many people struggle to purchase a residential home, let alone struggle to find a 25% down payment deposit to purchase an investment property. I understand this struggle. I was there.

I read books like this one, I attended conferences and seminars, I paid thousands for courses and information that have all contributed to my growth. However, I owe any success in property to the *'knowledge'* I acquired at Tafik's house.

It planted a seed in my mind and completely shifted my perspective on property. It opened me up to a *'possibility'*

I have come to accept that the person that acquires knowledge and utilises that knowledge often win the race.

Tafik's dad revelation completely changed my life. It taught me a universal truth in which I have adopted across every sphere of my life. 'Stay a student, become the master'. In simple terms, every successful person was once a student.

I wrote this book to do three things.

1. *Introduce you to a completely exciting high cash-flowing property strategy*
2. *Lay the foundations that anyone, can earn from property by just discovering what is possible.*
3. *Invite you to read this book with a completely open mind and of course, take action.*

This is your **discovery**.

I hope you catch the 'Ah ah or Eureka' moment and your perspectives changes just like when I caught my 'ah ha moment, from Tafik's dad.

"Every action triggers a reaction."
C. G. Watson

Introduction

Hey, I'm Tj.

Thank you for picking up my book. I am grateful that you did.

There are 100s of property books out there. Many of them promising you riches beyond your wildest imagination whilst only working 2 hours a month or others promising financial liberation in just 8 days. This isn't one of those. In fact, I want to hit some home truth before we get started.

The strategy I am about to teach you isn't easy. It's certainly not a get rich tomorrow scheme. It's important to know that if the information is embraced, it can create a significant income, a financial breakthrough and give you the ability to live your life on your own terms (travel more, reduce your working hours, quit your job or whatever that means to you)

I intended to make this book a little different, by spilling the bean on this very specific property strategy. I am not only going tell you how tens of thousands of people are changing their lives and income through property investing, but I will also show you the negative sides, the often unspoken about parts and the not so glamorous side of property investing through this strategy.

I would not want to pull the wool over your eyes by giving the impression that property investing is easy, but it can certainly be easier when you have the correct, relevant and undiluted facts at hand.

I wrote this book specifically as a way to bust some myths around the age old idea that starting a property business required years of experiences and most importantly, lots and lots of money.

This is quite frankly not the truth. The uninformed still believe this, however, the smart, information seeker, knowledge cravers, change 'wanters', financial freedom seekers, have to understand that there are 'many ways to skin a cat' (please note, no cats were skinned whilst writing this book)

Naturally, like any business, lots of experience and lots of funds is always helpful, but let's go on the premise that you don't have both. Should that stop you from tapping into the one market that is responsible for circa $468 billion generated by 173 billionaires? Of course it shouldn't.

Property investing has and will always be the go-to wealth creator for the ultra-wealthy. Hence why every person should work hard to add property to their income/wealth calculator.

Furthermore, Robert Watts who complies The Sunday Rich List every year once noted, that *"At least one in six people on the Sunday Times Rich List owes their wealth to property…"*.

I want to use this book to show you that it is possible to earn and build a property business by utilising this tiny little strategy, that does NOT require lots of money, that also does NOT require lots of experience or lots of time.

If I could factually demonstrate this to you. Would you start your property journey?

Why I wrote this book

The answer is simple. There is a lot of information out there on how you can "start in property", or "become a millionaire overnight through property", or "get financially free in 24 hours". There is certainly a lot of misinformation and hype out there. I wanted to show you a very BREXIT Proof solution, that does not require tons of money or a sophisticated understanding of property investing.

Why I really wrote this book

I want to give you as much introductory information on my go to strategy, so that one day when you are ready to start your journey as a property investor, you would consider my property training program as your start, grow and scaling option.

Who is this book for?

This book is for anyone that want to start a property business and build an income using the 'borrowed property' strategy. To take it a little further, it is to inspire you to think outside of the box and develop a solution driven mindset and never accept the terms, labels or preconceived ideas that your environment or yourself have created.

Who is this not for?

This book is certainly NOT for anyone looking for get rich quick opportunity. At my property events, I always ask my audience, 'if someone offers you £1 million pounds and all you had to do was to give them £1, how many people would do it? A handful of people always raise their hands. Please don't be like the handful that raise their hands. Because you will certainly lose your money. I over emphasise that while what I am about to teach you is not rocket science, you have to accept that effort, hard work, input is required to make money from property, business or in fact anything life changing.

An extra £2000 per month?

Could you do more, be more, give more if you have more?

What I am going to show you is certainly no get rich quick scheme or get rich tomorrow scheme. However, I want you to imagine a system that permits you to generate an additional income of £2k per month, but that is just the start.

You are about to discover a system that tens of thousands of entrepreneurs, intra-preneur and ordinary people are using to either boost their income, boost their pension or create a new life.

"Stop pointing fingers and placing blame on others. Your life can only change to the degree that you accept responsibility for it." - **Steve Maraboli**

The Problem

Save your money > Buy a property > Become a landlord > Rent it out > Rinse & Repeat

Starting a property business can seem impossible based on the often-limited information we have available.

Most new people to property investing are led to believe, through no significant fault of their own, but maybe through our parent, a lack of knowledge, or misinformation, that the only way to make money from property is to become a traditional property landlord who managed to save a 25% BTL deposit, who then buys a property and then rents it out.

If you are new to property, I am right? Was this also your impression?

Let us imagine you wanted to start a property business the 'traditional way' - *Save your money*

> Buy a property > Become a landlord > Rent it out > Rinse & Repeat

Let's look at the some really scary figures

I will use the London market for this example -

You saw an amazing property that you wanted to buy to rent out (i.e. become a traditional land-lord) –

The property value = £300,000

Deposit to acquire the property (25%) = £75,000 (**I have excluded Stamp Duty & Legal Costs**)

Do you have a £75,000 deposit? If not, can you save your way to £75,000.

Let's look at this way

Are you able to set aside £1000pm from your current income to save towards your £75,000 deposit?

Let's go a bit further
£1000 x 12 months = £12,000
£12,000 x 6 years = £72,000

£72,000 saved over 6 years to purchase the over £300,000 property

Now there are two further problems
1. No landlord or property owner is going to wait for you to save £72,000 over 6 years
2. The property market tends to rally every 6-10 years. Therefore the £300,000 property is likely to now be worth £330,000 or more.

This is often why many people fail to become property investors, simply because saving for a 25% Buy to Let deposit is often so difficult.

I have an alternative solution for you that will not require you to even buy a property, or saving for a mortgage deposit but yet still give you an income every month from a property that you 'control'.

The Opportunity

The 2018 hospitality market generated a total revenue of £17.8 Billion, with national and international brands such as Premier Inn, Holiday Inn, Crown Plaza and other popular hotel brand names leading the way in terms of guest occupancy and revenue. Hotels in London, Manchester and Edinburgh benefited from significant influx of tourism, corporates stays and overnight visits.

London - 19.8 Million visitors
Manchester - 1.3 Million visitors
Edinburgh - 2 Million visitors

Entire UK – 39.8 Million visitors

So why should you care about those 39.8 million visitors who spend circa £20 billion pounds annually, in fact why should you even consider the myriad of visitors and guests that stay in hotels like Premier Inn, Crown Plaza or the Intercontinental Hotel?

A better question might be, why should you care about 39.8 million visitors, £20 billion and your income?

Because in 2019, there is now a really crafty opportunity for the average entrepreneur to sneak in and claim a slice of the pie that hotels have coveted for centuries, simply because of the near impossible and extremely high barriers to entry.

What makes this opportunity even more interesting, is that anyone, quite literally anyone can claim a stake in the Crown Plaza or The Holiday Inn's turnover of nearly 4.9 billion pounds, without having to have any property experience, any hotel experience and not a lot of cash, and to make this opportunity even easier, the blueprint to copy them is now available in the chapters below.

Smart property entrepreneurs are starting their own boutique styled 'hotels' called Serviced Accommodation, which generates a similar return to a hotel room, without the same capital outlay as a hotel, but by simply copying and pasting what hotels have been doing for centuries.

Before we go any further let's look at some figures, for example if you wanted to start a 20 room hotel anywhere around the world. Here are some approximate figures (varies across the country and the world).

Company Registration - £40
Legal licenses and permits - £10,000
Opening and Marketing - £15,000
Land Purchase - £200,000 - £500,000
Hotel Build - £1,000,000
Furnishing - £100,000
Feasibility Report (Location Analysis, Room Rates, Occupancy Levels, Supply and Demand – 1% to 3%+ of build cost - £1000 to £3000
Miscellaneous – £10,000

= £1,336,040 to £1,638,040

£1,336,040 Divided by 20 rooms = £66,802 Per room set up

£1,638,040 Divided by 20 rooms = £81,902 Per room set up

Over the next few chapters I am going to show you what 100s of my clients and 1000s of smart property entrepreneurs have been doing over the last decade to get a piece of the 20 Billion Pound hotel action without the need to find, invest or borrow £1,336,040 to get started or more importantly invest between £66,802 or £81,902 to get started.

Your Property Mentor
Tj Atkinson

"Action speaks louder than words but not nearly as often."
— **Mark Twain**

How I got into this strategy

Mr Yussuf pulled me into his small home office. "Tj I have an opportunity for you".

Mr Yussuf was a rich man, any opportunity he offered, I was certain to grab it.

I thought, were he was going to ask me to assist him in some quick jobs, maybe deliver some leaflets for his many restaurants, or even drive a parcel from one side of London to the other side. Either way, whatever he was offering, I would be accepting it. I needed the money.

"Tj, my son is messing around and I want to teach him a lesson. Do you know how to manage properties?". I had recently read a quote by Richard Branson 'if someone offers you an amazing opportunity and you don't know how to do it, say yes, and figure it out later.

I immediately said YES.

I formulated a plan. I would quickly sign up to a course on how to become an estate agent.

I ran home, jumped on google and typed in 'how to become an estate agent'. As I scrolled through page one, something caught my attention.

<u>'List your property on Airbnb and earn **thousands** per month'.</u>

I run through the properties he had given me on the USB stick, found 8 properties that were currently empty and 2 which the tenancies were ending soon and listed them all on Airbnb.

By the end of the month. We had generated over £24,000. I transferred the money from Airbnb to Paypal, then to my bank account. I took out the cash and jumped on a bus to Mr Yussuf's house. I recall sliding the cash across the table to him. He sat there counting it and said £23,207. My rent roll if £16,000. Have you counted this?

"Yes, I counted it - I made it from some of the properties."

 "Some?

"Yes"

At that moment I remembered. He had given 20 properties. I had placed 8 on Airbnb, and I had forgotten to chase up on the rent on 12 other properties.

I assumed he was would be angry.

He jumped up and said "So you are saying is that, you have not collected ¾ of my rent". I looked at the ground and said no.

(Swear words *&%£) Tell me right now.....what you did...

I explained I had made around £3000 average per property. So £3000 x 8 = £24,000. I had spent some money on transportation, cleaning products, linen, etc.

He was stuck on the numbers... "so what you are saying is that £24,000 was made from these 8 properties, plus what due in rent from the other 12 properties". I said yes.

At that point, he said, don't tell anyone about this (Swear words *&%£ again), this is between you and I.

He took £3k cash and slid it across the table and said... "This is yours. Go and do it again." Which I did, over and over again.

What goes up must come down

The relationship eventually broke down. I went from having 20 properties generating over £50,000 per month to £0. Mr Yussuf eventually took his properties back.

I was back to zero properties and zero pounds. However, this was a moment of change for me.

I had seen how I could use someone's asset, with their permission, I could re-rent out their property and make a few thousands per month.

I had had a taste and wanted more.

I called every estate agent and every landlord and begged to rent their property for this purpose.

How I started again

My first agent was a guy called Ray. Ray said, I don't understand what you are asking for. I blabbed on and blabbed on.

"Are you asking for a flat that you can sublet?"

I kept quiet and then said 'kinda'.

Ray was the first agent to hand me over a property in Docklands, London. He said come into the office and I can show you a few properties that some of my landlords might be interested in allowing you to sublet.

Subletting

I quizzed Ray. How come you keep using the word subletting. I had shied away from that from as I had thought 'subletting' was illegal. I assumed what I did with Mr Yussuf was something called 'Airbnbing'. Ray said, there is nothing illegal about subletting as long as it is legal.

Have you ever thought subletting was illegal? Most people do. Well, its factually incorrect. Ray was correct. Illegal subletting is illegal, whereas permitted subletting is perfectly legal.

Subletting II

Effectively, this business is not subletting as we are not assigning the contract to another person under an AST. But YES, technically, for argument sake, the general understanding of 'subletting' is renting a flat to re-rent (which is what we do)

"Belief means nothing without actions"
— **Randa Abdel-Fattah**

The Copy Cat Model (Samwer Brothers)

My VERY Simple Business and Investment strategy

Find someone who is doing what you want to do and COPY them. I know you might have been expecting a technical break down or analysis of the property market but that is my simple business and investment strategy.

I am simply referring to the *copy-cat* model. I came across 3 brothers a few years ago and it completely changed my perspective on business. I had to accept that I was no Thomas Edison or Alexander Graham Bell. I respect inventors and innovators, but I didn't have the idea, money or time to create. I didn't have the desire to make mistakes and more mistakes until I eventually got it right, like Thomas Edison, who failed with the lightbulb over 1000 times. Well done to him but I needed to find a quicker way to success.

The Samwer Brothers have built up an incredible business model (Rocket Internet) which simply copies successful businesses, models and systems. Although, they have faced many criticisms for their style, it has brought a net worth of over 2.2 billion euros for the three brothers.

The Samwer brother realised the power of emulation. To emulate simply means to match or surpass (a person or achievement), typically by imitation.

Benefits of Emulation

1. **Leverage Experience**
2. **Leverage Mistakes**
3. **Discover a missing niche**
4. **Double down on a niche**

This is simply what I teach my success students - How to copy the ever- booming hotel industry. Learn from their mistakes, leverage their experience, customers and model and build our businesses on their back.

This reduces our failure rate and significantly increases our chances of success.

"Your life is a print-out of your thoughts."
— Steve Maraboli

Rent 2 Rent (R2R) - Let's get straight into it

What is Rent to Rent – Rent to Rent is a highly popular property strategy. In simple terms, it's the ability to gain **control** of a property to use for a property business, without the need to purchase the property from the legal owner.

Rent to Rent is simply renting, managing or joint venturing with the property owner with the intent to 're-rent' that property out in order to take a margin, a slice or a percentage.

For example, a smart property investors might rent a property from an agent or landlord and with the agent's or landlord's permission, they could turn that property into an income generator by utilising what we in the industry called R2SA also known as Rent to Serviced Accommodation.

Can you start a property business without much money! YES!

How?

By becoming the 'Middle Wo[man].'

This is how the 'Middle Wo[man]' wins by using the Rent to Rent Serviced Accommodation system.

a) The property owner has laid out a 25% deposit to purchase a property (which they intend to rent out)
b) You rent the property from the property owner or agent and offer to pay his/her rent (Using a guaranteed rent, management or Joint Venture model)
c) You take 'control' of the property
d) You 're-rent' this property (per night) to the 39.8 million people who travel into the United Kingdom every year.
e) You keep the difference between the rent you pay the landlord, costs and profit generated.
f) Rinse and Repeat

Let's try a more practical example (Approximate figure Ex: Fees and taxes)

Landlord (Legal Property Owner)
Purchase Property £300,000 25% Deposit = £75,000 Rent Generated = £1500pm x 12 months x 5 years = £90,000

(You) Rent to Serviced Accommodation
Rental £1500pm Rental Deposit = £1500 Your Income = £500pm x 12 months x 5 years = £30,000

This is why so smart entrepreneurs are flooding into the Rent to Rent Serviced Accommodation market.

A) The landlord as shown above is happy with their investment of **£75,000** and is delighted with his £90,000 rental return in rental return over 5 years.

B) On the other hand, the property entrepreneur is happy with their 'investment' in renting the landlord's property and is elated with a £30,000 profit over a 5 year period on a property that they do not even own.

Please bear in mind the owner of the property will also benefit from capital appreciation, which you will not, but you have then ask yourself this question.... Does it matter!

The benefit of Rent to Serviced Accommodation is that you get to utilise someone else's asset to increase your income and help you build your purchase deposit significantly faster.

What is Serviced Accommodation (Also highly known as R2SA or Serviced Apartments)

Serviced Accommodation is exactly as the name suggests. It's the provision of services in an accommodation. Think about an apartment with hotel-style amenities. Such as the provision of house-keeping, WIFI and a number of other services for the guests. Bills, taxes, utilities are generally inclusive of the prices charged per night.

A Serviced Accommodation can be a studio, 1, 2 or 3 bed Apartment or a house, where you charge the arriving guests a rate per night.

Guests and clients can stay for 1 day to up to 6 months and in some cases, a little longer.

Serviced Apartment/House #1 – Providing whole apartments or houses with hotel-style amenities to different people within a whole house

Serviced Room #2 – Providing a room or rooms with hotel-style amenities within your own home. (If you have a spare room in your home, you should certainly consider opening your doors to welcome holiday makers in for a small nightly fee like thousands of people are currently doing.

For the purpose of this book, we will focus on Serviced Apartment or Serviced houses (meaning whole occupation, rather than part occupation)

We are seeing a significant influx of people flooding into Serviced Accommodation, because the market place is proven. The Accommodation Industry in 2018 turnover was £28 Billion, this means, that is a huge opportunity, for new entrants to take a small slice of the pie. At my Introduction to Property events, I always ask my audience a simply question, which I am going to ask you now...

Out of a £28 billion pound pie, even with no experience, do you think it is possible for you to take £36,000 out of a £28 billion pie?

ACCOMMODATION INDUSTRY TURNOVER IN THE UK 2018

28 bn GBP

SPENDING ON ACCOMMODATION SERVICES IN THE UK IN 2018

26.5m GBP

AVERAGE WEEKLY EXPENDITURE ON ACCOMMODATION SERVICES IN THE UK

10.90 GBP

"If your actions don't live up to your words, you have nothing to say."

Who are the big players in the Serviced Accommodation arena

(Operators generating over £1million a year from this strategy)

Bridgestreet – https://www.bridgestreet.com

Go Native - https://www.nativemanagement.co.uk

Staycity – www.staycity.com

Marlin Apartments – www.marlin.com

www.fraserhospitality

https://www.sacoapartments.com/

Why would a landlord give you their property?

Let's look at this example again

Landlord (Legal Property Owner)
Purchase Property £300,000 25% Deposit = £75,000 Rent - £1500pm x 12 months x 5 years = £90,000

(You) Rent to Serviced Accommodation
Rental £1500pm Deposit = £1500 Income - £500pm x 12 months x 5 years = £30,000

I have been asked this question numerous times. "Why would a landlord or property owner willingly give his or her property to a Serviced Accommodation operator".

Many people find it hard to understand why a landlord who is making an income or has bought a property would give their property to someone else so that someone else can also make an income.

I want you to remember that the landlord will still receive their rental income as they were previously doing in the example above, they will now benefit from having a company or professional operator who will look after their property and maintain the property to an agreed standard.

When speaking to a landlord or an estate agent, be sure to remind them that the nature of your Serviced Accommodation business means that the property will be professionally cleaned, professionally managed and professionally maintained, which means that when the property is return after the end of the contract, the landlord will not need to spend money and time refurbishing the property.

Here are a few more reason a landlord will be willing to give you their property –

1. Tired – The landlord may be tired of managing the property for a number of reasons

2. Fed up – The landlord is fed up of chasing rent or dealing with tenants

3. Desire to be passive – The landlord would much rather not have an active role in his/her property, but would much rather just collect their rent

4. Want to retire or travel – The landlord wishes to spend more time travelling or spending more time with their partners or loved one

My secret sauce for deals

If you want an influx of deals. Focus on building long term relationships with your landlords or your estate agents.

One of my first deal turned into 20 plus deals and a second business, because I did something that most people fail to do.

I recall a call to James' office. I was looking for a property for my serviced accommodation business.

James explained that the specific property I called about would not be suitable as the landlord had asked for specific type of tenant.

In order to build *'good will'* with James. I asked him if I could help him find a tenant for that property. I ran around asking multiple people if they wanted to rent a flat in Catford, London and eventually a friend recommended someone and I simply passed this tenant to James. James was able to let the property quickly, impress his land-lord and secure his management fee.

I want you to do something, lead with value always. Find a way to add value to your landlords and agents (for free) and watch how they return the favour.

Up till today, James still calls me and offers my any suitable serviced accommodation properties across the country first before he puts it on the open market.

This one relationship, birth a second business. Deal Packaging.

I once read a book by Robert Cialdini, where he breaks down 6 key methods for influence. This one book changed my life, it taught me about what has now become my favourite word and go to strategy. ***Reciprocity***.

The term reciprocity simply means, if you lead with value, if you do something for someone, they become morally obliged to return the favour.

Science recognises this as *cause and effect*, Christian understand this as the *law of sowing and reaping*, Buddhist call this *Karma*. If we accept this as truth, then we ought to change how we do business. If you understand that giving will, by natural order bring back business, it stops us from been selfish or greedy but helps us to focus on helping, whilst knowing that the favour will be returned.

My relationship with James has generated multiple 6 figures, it's created jobs. It's change my clients and staff's lives, and help us grow our property business faster.

Benjamin Franklin once quoted, 'no one cares how much you know, until they know how much you care'. If you want an abundance of deals or landlords and agents offering you property, find a way to add value to them.

(Dwayne)

A client of mine could not pass referencing nor could they access a suitable guarantor; so we formulated a plan using my secret sauce. He would simply offer to add value to an agent. This one action has led to an agent handing my client over the agent's personal property to use as serviced accommodation. Dwayne simply offered to do a viewing for the agent when the agent hinted that he was overwhelmed with a staff sickness.

Dwayne called me crying over the phone. The agent has said 'no one had ever offer to help him before, and therefore he would like to do something for Dwayne. A few days later the agent told Dwayne, that they simply could not give him a property to rent because according to their terms they had to reference the company or individual, however, he understood Dwayne would not pass referencing, so when the agent's personal property became available 2 month later, he passed it over to Dwayne. Dwayne now has 3 Serviced Accommodation units based on my secret sauce.

Look I am not saying it works all time, what I am asking you to do, is to formulate the habit of leading with value if you want to start and scale your property business using someone else's asset.

What type of people use Serviced Accommodation

– Customers & Clients

1. Contractors – Construction workers and Team members
2. Corporates – Business Travellers
3. Leisure – Family Holiday makers
4. *Bleisure* – Business Travellers who mix work and leisure
5. Groups – Large group who desire to travel and stay together

In order to ensure that you maximise your nightly income, work on a plan to attract as many of the *5 types of Serviced Accommodation user* to book and rent your Serviced Accommodation.

Serviced Accommodation has changed over the last few years. Most new entrants into the market look at Serviced Accommodation as the provision of short term accommodation for

Number 3
Number 5

However, the more experienced operators understand that by actively targeting all 5 users, you have more visibility, more exposure and therefore more bookings, which translates into more income for you.

What types of properties that work for Serviced Accommodation?

Contractors	**2 bedroom+**
Corporate/Business Travellers	**Studio to 2 Bedroom+**
Leisure	**Studio to 2 Bedroom+**
Bleisure	**Studio to 2 Bedroom+**
Group	**2 Bedroom to 4/5 Bedroom+**

**Caution

As we begin to see changes and greater regulation in the Serviced Accommodation arena, it is vital to ensure that you do not rely on one clients type, but focus on developing networks and access to the the above 5.

Brexit, Coronavirus and unexpected problems which affect tourists and leisure guests could affect your cashflow, however, smart serviced accommodation operators are ensuring that they are protecting their business by ensuring they also market heavily to Contractors and Corporate client types.

"Actions always have consequences!"
— Joel Coen

Protect the Asset

This is important. As you have previously read, you are 'borrowing' someone else's property.

This means we are taking '*control*' of someone's hard earned asset. There are a few factors that could easily affect the running of your property business, which in turn could affect the owner's property.

As you become 'a small boutique hotel', you are likely to face similar issues that hoteliers face, for example, *Partying, Escorting and in some cases prostitution*. There are dozens of ways to mitigate these issue from occurring, however, it would be irresponsible for me not to inform you about these things.

Your main job as a Rent to Serviced Accommodation operator is to protect the asset. Which means ensuring that protecting the Landlord's asset is significantly more important than your profit.

This mindset will serve you in the long term.

Some of the common issue we face in this business involves *partying*.

Example #1

In 2017, we rented one of our 3 bed penthouse to two young men. I recall meeting them to facilitate their checking in on Friday and would meet them on Sunday morning to inspect the property and perform a check-out. On Sunday morning, just before church, I went to the property, the front door was wide open. The property had been trashed, my television screen broken, the curtain railing ripped off the wall and lastly blood on the ceiling in the master bedroom. Cutting the story short, we were able to recoup our losses and £6k damages.

But this situation caused significant trouble with our neighbours and building management.

Example #2

2017 we rented 3 brand new properties in Aldgate East (London). The guest had a mid-week party, destroying multiple apartments and causing over £40k in damages.

This resulted in our contracts been terminated and losing our deposits of over £10k.

There are now new and robust strategies we have developed in order to secure and protect our landlord's assets.

These sort of damage and problem affect the industry and landlord's perception of the business, which leads to a reduction in willing landlords that would grant us their properties to be used for Serviced Accommodation.

If you intend on generating an income from other people's assets, then you have to set your company objective to looking after the landlord's asset first, profit second.

I wanted this book to serve as a true reflection of this business. I feel it is important to know the issues associated with this business rather than gaslight you to thinking life is a big bunch of roses.

There is no point telling you how you can make £1k profit per month but not telling you about the potential issues that every single business face.

With smart, robust systems we have completely reduced any potential issues, this comes with experience and understanding and developing robust check in processes.

If these issues have put you off, then good. If you accept that every business has circumventable issues then carry on.

Location
Where does Serviced Accommodation work?

The truthful answer is..... NOT EVERYWHERE.

There are certain quick-fire indicators whether your Serviced Accommodation will work. One quick way would be to look at the level of hotel activity in your chosen area.

Remember, a hotel investment into an area is based on quantifiable figures and thousands of pounds or dollars in Research (Feasibility Study). If there are no signs, or extremely low signs of hotel activity and investment in that area, then walk away

Have a look here – Look at their level of bookings/reservations in the last 6 to 24 hours....

Park Plaza Westminster Bridge London ★★★★

Fabulous
15,280 reviews **8.6**

Location 9.4

Show prices

Lambeth, London · Show on map · 0.2 miles from "London SE1 7PB, UK"
Metro access

Located on the South Bank of the Thames, Park Plaza Westminster Bridge
London is set opposite the Houses of Parliament and Big Ben, on the South
Bank.

Booked 11 times in the last 1 hour on our site

Clayton Hotel Birmingham ★★★★

Birmingham City Centre, Birmingham · Show on map

The 4-star Clayton Hotel Birmingham is just a 5-minute walk from the Bullring
Shopping Centre. It serves modern food in its stylish restaurant.
Booked 13 times in the last 6 hours on our site

Jurys Inn Birmingham ★★★★

Birmingham City Centre, Birmingham · Show on map

This modern Jurys Inn is in Birmingham city centre, within 150 metres of the
International Convention Centre and the Arena Birmingham.
Booked 31 times in the last 6 hours on our site

What about if you are the first one in the area? Walk away.

Location is paramount in Serviced Accommodation. Some of the quickest and simplest way to determine whether your location will work for your serviced accommodation business is to use the following websites.

1. Booking.com
2. Airbnb.com
3. Tripadvisor.com
4. Airdna.co

Use the top 3 website (OTA) to see what local hotels, competitors and serviced operators are currently charging

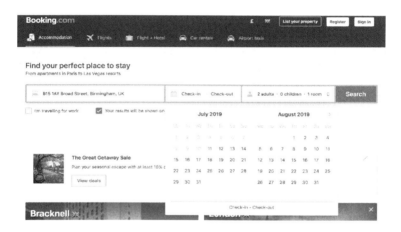

Another quickfire location analysis –

Determine which of the 4 below are prominent in your desired location

Types of people that use Serviced Accommodation

Mark as appropriate for your location. If you score 2 out of 5 then the location might be worth a deeper analysis.

1. Con-tractors	Yes	No
2. Tourists	Yes	No
3. Corpor-ates	Yes	No
4. Groups	Yes	No
5. Bleisure	Yes	No

For example – London
Determining whether a property in **London** might work for you

1. C o n-tractors	Yes (Y)	No
2. Tourists	Yes (Y)	No
3. Corpor-ates	Yes (Y)	No
4. Groups	Yes (Y)	No
5. Bleisure	Yes (Y)	No

For example – Liverpool
Determining whether a property in **Liverpool**
might work for you

1. Con-tractors	Yes	No (N)
2. Tourists	Yes (Y)	No
3. Corpor-ates	Yes	No (N)
4. Groups	Yes	No (N)
5. Bleisure	Yes	No (N)

Other methods to analyse a location

1. **Airbnb**
2. **Tripadvisor**
3. **Airdna**

Listing your property on Airbnb and booking.-com

Airbnb.com

Listing your property on Airbnb is relatively easy and rather seamless. Airbnb will ask for information pertaining to your property in order to get it listed and active so you can start receiving bookings.

This information typically includes, address, style of property (house, apartment, boat, etc), configuration of the property and amenities.

Make sure your listing is accurate. As one wrong listing or what could be deemed as misinformation could land you in some serious trouble. I recall listing of one of our studio apartments a while ago.

We mistakenly listed this property as having two room rather than two beds. When the guest arrive, she immediately filed a complaint with

Airbnb, that she had booked the apartment because she had needed two separate rooms and clearly this was not the case. Airbnb immediately found her an alternative property and refunded her, meaning we were out of pocket for that specific booking. Please note, if your property has a bath, do not mistakenly list it as a shower, or if your property has no WIFI, make sure you stipulate you do not have WIFI.

Airbnb is typically quick to verify your property and you can start getting guests pretty much immediately.

Make sure your calendar is up to date.

Booking.com

Booking.com is significantly different to Airbnb when it comes to listing your property. A few years ago, booking.com introduced verification processes to list your property on their website. Please pay close attention to this. If you are brand new, this is very much likely to affect you.

In order to ensure that the properties listed on their platform[s] are honest and permissible, they introduced a scheme, where they will send you a 10 digit code in the post to the address of the property you will be using for your Serviced Accommodation business. Please note, this code will not be sent to your residence address but the business address.

Once this code is received, you are able to input the code into booking.com website and activate your account. This does not happen all the time, but is likely to occur when you list a brand new property. This offers booking.com some reassure that you have access to that property.

Booking.com will typically require you to use brightly lit pictures, provide detailed information about the property, such as full address, amenities.

Photography

Your photo will make or break your ability to generate an income in Serviced Accommodation. Make you to do NOT use your iphone or take the pictures yourself. You can find suitable photographers on gumtree or Facebook.com. It is important that you only use a photographer that is an expert with interior shots. This means they understand lighting and space. An interior photographer know how to make the space look and feel larger and spacious. This is crucial to gain customers over your competitors.

Live examples of our Serviced Accommodation properties

Waterloo (London)

Rent from Landlord £1400
Re-rent to our guests at £160pn x 24 nights (Avr) = £3840pm

Maida Vale (London)

Rent from Landlord £1500
Re-rent to our guests at £135pn x 21 nights
(Avr) = £2835pm

Canary Wharf (London)

Rent from Landlord £1900
Re-rent to our guests at £170pn x 21 nights
(Avr) = £3910pm

Where to find suitable properties

Rightmove

rightmove

Zoopla

Realistic Costs of starting a Rent to Rent Serviced Accommodation business

These examples will vary across the world

a) 1 Month Rent in Advance
b) 4 to 6 Weeks Deposit (Refundable)
c) Agents/Landlords Fee
d) Referencing Fees

A general example in United Kingdom, Birmingham

a) £850 (Rent in Advance) (Fully Furnished)
b) £785 - £1178 (4 to 6 week deposit)
c) ~~£300 (Agency Fees)~~
d) £250 (Referencing Fees)
e) £1000 (Soft Furnishing)
Totalling = £2885/£3278

Let's look back at the cost of setting up a hotel room (suite) at £66,802 Versus £2885/£3278

Yes, of course, the hotel will benefit from brand growth or they might have a 20/30 year growth plan, but I want you to imagine the benefit of setting up a 'boutique' apartment at only £2885/£3278.

Let's try another example in London

a) £1750 (Rent in Advance)
b) £1616 - £2424 (4 to 6 week deposit)
c) ~~£300 (Agency Fees)~~
d) £250 (Referencing Fees)
e) £1000 (Soft Furnishing)

Totalling = £4616/ £5424

Ps: In many cases, you are able to negotiate NOT paying a 4 to 6 week deposit to the property owner or the agent. This is always a bonus.

Let's look at the cost of starting a Serviced Accommodation business in Birmingham and

London again, minus the 4 to 6 damage deposit

Birmingham = £2100
London = £3000

Case Study – Staycity

Staycity - https://www.staycity.com

Number of Apartments 1,497

Locations –

Dublin (179 apartments)
Edinburgh (146)
Manchester (84)
Liverpool (56)
Birmingham Arcadian Centre (79)
Birmingham Newhall Square (170)
London Heathrow (269)
London Greenwich (161)
Paris (50)
Marseille (108)
York (190)
Lyon (144)
London Covent Garden (106)

2018 – Turnover = €70 million
2017 – Turnover = €60 million

Their growth plan to reach revenues of €500 million by 2022 and ultimately seeking a stock market floatation.

Case Study – Saco Apartments

Saco Apartment - https://www.sacoapartments.com

Number of Apartments 80,000
We are a leading hospitality business offering serviced apartment
Accommodation in over 200 locations
In over 50 countries worldwide.
350 employees in the UK and 14 in the Netherlands.
A global annual turnover of circa £41 million.
80,000 stylish serviced apartments in over 260 destinations worldwide

Why Corporates and Companies choose Serviced Accommodation over hotels

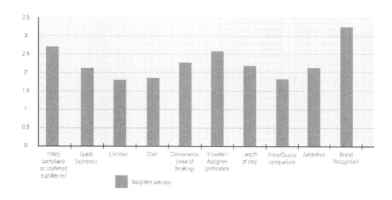

According to The Apartment Services, brand recognition and Preferred Supplier List (PSL) are the main attractions for corporates and companies. If you want to consistently attract corporate booking focus on developing your brand recognition as indicated in the image above.

Corporate booking are golden opportunity for a number of reason.

1. They tend to be longer term or a few night per week across a long duration. This is significant as it guarantees your income over that period
2. No additional fees to acquire the customers
3. No credit card processing fees as they typically pay on invoice

If you want more corporate businesses to use your Serviced Accommodation, then make sure you address the issue pointed out below.

Further research shows that one of the main reasons that the hotel industry services many of the corporate booking is due to 6 main points, with 'Shortage of apartments in required locations' and the 'booking process does not take too long'

Hotels make the booking process seamless and therefore better suited for the busy guest.

Quick Tip to win Corporate bookings: Make your website, your booking and process as smooth and seamless as possible

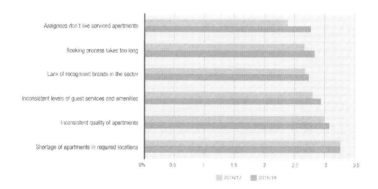

Can I show you how and why smart property entrepreneurs are flooding into the Serviced Accommodation market?

1. With 20+ million overnight visitors visiting the United Kingdom
2. With those visitors spending over £21 Billion Pounds in hotels
3. With Corporates switching from hotel to Serviced Accommodation

This has created a great opportunity for normal people like you and I, to take advantage of the Rent to Rent model and pick up some Serviced Accommodation property to take our slice of the £21 Billion Pound pie.

Let look at this figure below

Scenario 1 - Hotel (a)

Hotel in London - A family of 4 are visiting London for 2 Nights

150 Per Night (2 PAX) over 2 Nights = 300 (Room 1)
150 Per Night (2 PAX) over 2 Nights = 300 (Room 2)

Subtotal Stay Cost = £600
Restaurant (4 Persons), WIFI, Spaces = £30x4 equals £120

Total Hotel Stay over 2 nights = **£720**

Scenario 2 - Serviced Accommodation (b)

Serviced Accommodation   in London - A family of 4 are visiting London for 2 Nights

£150 Per Night (4 PAX) over 2 Nights = £300

Feeding (4 PAX) = £10x4 equals £40 (Oven, Cooker, Microwave)

Total SA Stay = **£340**

Why should you start a Rent to Rent Serviced Accommodation business?

Let us go back to the example above –

Company Registration - £100
Legal expenses to obtain licenses and permits – £10,000
Grand Opening and Marketing – £15,000
Land Purchase – £500,000
Hotel Build – £800,000 to £1,000,000
Furnishing – £100,000
Feasibility Report (Location Analysis, Room Rates, Occupancy Levels, Supply and Demand – 1% to 3%+ of build development cost - £8000
Miscellaneous – £10,000

= £1,443,100

Whereas with the Rent to Rent Serviced Accommodation System you have the complete advantage over a small or large boutique hotel. Let us crunch some real number for some of our Serviced Accommodation properties -

FIGURES -

£950 Rent – Southampton (Furnished)
£125 x 23 Nights = £2875

Minus all costs = £2267.50

Profit = £607.50 per month

£1210 Rent – Birmingham (Furnished)
£145 x 21 Nights = £3045

Minus all costs = £2658.10

Profit = £636.90 per month

£1500 Rent – London (Furnished)
£165 x 21 = £3465

Minus all costs = £ 2923.70

Profit = £541.30 per month

You don't have to be great to start, but you have to start to be great.
- *Joe Sabah*

What should your Serviced Accommodation look like

Legal & Regulations

As a hotel has a number of responsibilities and follow underlying legislation and regulation, as Serviced Accommodation operators we have to take into account some of these rules also.

There are not many laws surrounding Serviced Accommodation specifically, however, it pays to pay attention to the model we emulate, which is the hotel industry.

Things to consider:

Food Safety / Hygiene

Guest Registration

Health & Safety

Electrical Appliance Testing (PAT)

Fire Risk Assessment required to comply with the Regulatory Reform (Fire Safety) Order 2005

Planning Permission / Change of use (If required)

TV Licensing (other licenses also required if pre-recorded music or films are played or shown to the public)

Licenses for serving alcohol to the public, live music, special events etc.

Hotel Proprietors Act

Data Protection Act **2018**

Consumer Protection from Unfair Trading Regulations 2008 (is your advertising completely transparent, truly reflecting the product on offer)

Equality Act 2010 - (accessibility and discrimination)

Public Liability Insurance – Evidence that Public Liability Cover is maintained, prior to assessment you will be asked to upload your certificate of insurance as evidence

ICO registration

Rules to follow

London Specific (ONLY)
London - Deregulation Bill

Taking into consideration the importance to London of its tourism industry and the rise of short-letting organisations such as Airbnb, the Government considered that the provisions were restrictive so decided to remove them in sections 44 & 45 of the Act. These revisions will come into force on 26 May 2015.

Section 44 of the Act amends the 1973 Act to make it clear that the use of residential property as temporary sleeping accommodation in Greater London does not represent a material change of use requiring planning permission if:

(i) the aggregate number of nights during a calendar year for which the property is used as temporary sleeping accommodation is not greater than 90 days

Will we see greater regulation outside of London? Most likely…

Quick Fire – Answering my most asked questions

Quick Fire Questions

Hi Tj,

What is the best way to get started?

There are a number of ways to get started in Serviced Accommodation. Larger Serviced Accommodation operators usually own their own developments or use the Lease model.
The smaller operators like you and I usually use the following 3 models –

Rent 2 Rent
This is proving to be one of the most popular ways to start a Serviced Accommodation business. It allows for smart entrepreneurs to rent a property from a landlord, agent or developer and re-rent the same property out to short term guests.

You can get Rent to Rent properties directly from Landlords or through Estate Agents.

Management
This model is when you take on the management of a property to use a Serviced Accommodation from the owner. You will operate the property as a SA from a management stance.

You can get Rent to Rent Serviced Accommodation properties directly from Landlords

Joint Venture
This model is also very popular with smart property entrepreneurs. Using the Joint Venture model allows you as the operator to JV with the property owners. This simply means that you and the landlords (property owner) split the costs and profits generated from the business

You can get Rent to Rent Serviced Accommodation properties directly from Landlords

Hi Tj,

How do I make money from this strategy?

Location Matters!

1. Not every single location works as a serviced accommodation property. Always consider the 5 types of clients and determine whether at least one of them visit that specific area and how frequently. Ideally, just like a hotel, you should target major towns and cities as you are likely to serve 1 to 5 of the clients. Always rank your analysis based on how many of the client types you will be able to attract.

Platforms

2. Use Platforms like Airdna.co and other Online Travel Agents (Booking.com, Airbnb etc.

Making Extra Cash

3. Opt in for Tiered Pricing, which simply means you will be able to set a standard rate per night, however, with the tiered pricing, you are also able to set an additional cost per night once your standard PAX has been met. For example, you may charge £100 per night for 4 people, however, if 6 people book your accommodation, then you can charge an additional £10 for the 5 people, an additional £10 for the 6 person, therefore increasing your true nightly rate to £120 per night.

4. Include a sofabed where you can. This always add value to your offer

Hi Tj,
I don't have the funds to get started!

It can cost anything from £800 to £6,000 to get started. In some cases, you may not have the initial start-up capital. Consider using the Joint Venture (JV) Option.

With the rate of inflation at 2.4% and Interest Rate at less than 1%. If any of your friends and family have money sitting in a bank they are effectively losing money.

Here are typical ways of raising funds from family or friends for your property business

£5k in the bank earning 1% (Let's not factor inflation) = £50 return per year
Based on the average figures such as

£1210 Rent – Birmingham (Furnished)
£145 x 21 Nights = £3045

Minus all costs = £2658.10

Profit = £636.90 per month

If your friend or family was currently earning £50 per year on their savings. You could offer a Joint venture or loan agreement.

On a joint venture agreement, you might split the £636.90 50/50, which means your JV partner will get back £318.45pm x 12 months = £3,821.

On a Loan Agreement, you might offer a simple return of 10% – 12% per year

Hi Tj,

What types of properties can I rent for my Serviced Accommodation business?

Many leasehold buildings, mainly apartments will not permit the use of short term rentals. Whereas many houses may not have such prohibitions in place.

Look out for such clauses in the leases and always take caution to read the leases properly before renting such a unit for your Serviced Accommodation business.

Hi Tj,
Should I self-managed or give the property to a Management company?

You have the option of managing your own Serviced Accommodation or using a management company, who will run and manage the entire process for you.

Management companies can charge 10 to 20% from what is generated from your Serviced Accommodation.

One of the benefits of using a Management company means, you can invest or rent a Serviced Accommodation in high yielding locations even if you do not live nearby.

For example, if you lived in Swindon, you could benefit from Birmingham's busy footfall by hiring a management company to run, organise and manage the entire business for you.

Or Alternatively you can use a lockbox or Key-safe

Hi Tj,
How do I get my 1st property?

Working with agents

There are various ways to get your first Serviced Accommodation property. The easiest way is simply to work directly with Landlords (D2V) or go through estate agents

What to consider when working with agents

Affordability & Referencing – Estate Agents will perform affordability and referencing checks.

It is very likely that they will want to do a reference on your business. In many cases, your business might new and will not have 2 or 3 year accounts that most agents desire.

In this situation many agents will require you as the individual to stand as a guarantor for your company. What this simple means is that if your business does not pay the rent, then you as the individual are liable.

Some agents might require you to pay 3 to 6 months rent upfront. This is usually as a form of security for them and it ensures that they are protected for that duration.

The benefit to you is that you will not need to pay any rent over that duration, conversely, paying 3 to 6 month upfront might be rather cash intensive.

Adverse credit – If you know you have adverse credit, such as CCJ or Bankruptcy, these should not stop your working with an agent. It might mean you need to more creative. This means, you might have to bring on a JV partner.

Make sure you let the agent know you have adverse credit before a credit or referencing check is carried out or you could lose your initial/holding fee.

Always ask the agent what is typical referencing process before you put down any money to hold or secure a property

Building Trust

Estate Agents typically have 2 forms of trainings. One is standard AST (Assured Shorthold Tenancy) or Sales Training.

Your job is to convince the agent why they should deviate from their current training or understand and work with you.

It's important to make sure your agent understands the benefits associated with working with you for the purpose of running your Serviced Accommodation versus a normal tenancy.

Building Trust
- KYP or KYP (Know your Product or Know you Service)
- Have a credible website
- Incentivise
- Add value to them

Hi Tj,
Should I work with a Sourcer?

A property sourcer is someone that goes out to the marketplace and find, packages and delivers a deal to you for a fee.

These fees can range from £1000 to £5000. In many cases, I suggest you try and secure some deals yourself first and if you find that you are not able to confidently persuade an agent or landlord to work with you, then it may make sense to use a credible sourcer.

Why do people use sourcers
1. They do not have the skill set to negotiate
2. They do not have the time to call 100's of agents and landlord
3. Time Precious investors
4. Hands off investors

Why it makes sense to pay a sourcer a fee –

The sourcer does most of the leg work.

They will have to spend time and money on marketing and if they find a you a deal that potentially looks like the example below then you should be excited about paying them.

Example
Profit of £700 per month x 12 months x 3 year agreement = £25,200.

If someone found you a deal that generated that generated £25,200 over a 3 year period would you have a problem paying them a fee of £2000?

Hi Tj,

How much should I spend on prepping the property/refurbishment?

I do not usually encourage taking on properties that require much work. The notion of using the Rent to Serviced Accommodation strategies means you should try and get into the business with as little funds as possible.

In some cases where the deal is very attractive, but requires some refurbishing, then I suggest a maximum invest of 1 month profit. For example, if the property will yield around £700 per month, then I would suggest a maximum of £700 is spent on the refurb.

Quick Tip: If you plan to do some refurbishing work to the owners/landlords property, try and negotiate a reduction in rent or a rent free period to offset the funds you have spent on the owner's property.

Hi Tj,
Can I insure the property?

Yes, you should absolutely insure the property, using the right and relevant insurance product.

Get insurances Specialist insurance

- Buildings Cover for rebuild or repair to your property following an insured event (Fires, Storm, Malicious damage etc)

- Contents Cover for loss or damage to contents within your properties

- Public Liability Cover for liability to tenants, guests and third parties for injury, illness or damage to their property arising from your property.

- Employers Liability Cover for liability to employees for illness or injury sustained in the course of working for you in relation to your serviced accommodation.

- Business Interruption Cover for your loss of income should the property be uninhabitable due to buildings and/or contents damage covered by the policy.

- Types of let We can arrange cover in respect of various types of holiday let including Airbnb, owner occupied with rooms let as holiday accommodation and 'rent-to-rent'.

Hi Tj,

I loved this book and I would love to go to the next step?

I offer a training and mentoring program. You can reach out to me www.tjatkinson.com and sign up for our Advantage Serviced Accommodation Program

Feel free to join my free resource FB page - https://www.facebook.com/groups/170205463387522/

Feel free to join my instagram – https://www.instagram.com/tjalife

Feel free to connect via linkedin - https://www.linkedin.com/in/tj-atkinson12345

Testimonials & Reviews

Here is a list of 100s of people I have trained and what they have to say about my Serviced Accommodation Advantage Training program...

Denzel Ndlovu

It was amazing. Honestly walked out with a much more better understanding of how to operate an SA , especially since I only started looking at the strategy this year (2020).It was definitely worth it highly recommend it

Ashley Stewart

I attended the SA course last week and absolutely loved it. Full of great content, not just the positives, but the negatives/risks that you can encounter. Didn't ever feel like I was being sold to or the strategy being made to seem like something it's not. Highly recommend!

Charlotte Grace-Gordon

I attended the SA Training course that TJ ran back in December and have to say it was really impressive. There was so much content and he went into a lot of detail. He will not leave the room until every person understands fully what he is teaching no matter how long it takes. He not only tells you about the good stuff with the business but warns you about the bad stuff that he experienced on his journey and tells you of ways to avoid the same things happening to you. You will get so much invaluable information. His course is a must for anyone thinking of going into this business.

Nicole Mariza

Brutally honest, eye opening, fantastic delivery of valuable information and personal experience!...
It's up to you what you do with it afterwards. Plus, you have full support if you need it.
Thank you TJ.

Kabir Habib Bakht

Tj is not like any other trainer i have met and i have been to a ton!!! He tells you the truth no upsell!! He answered every question i had about SA literally everything!!! Highly recommend him!! He gives you everything contracts SA calculator how to analyse the deal ect. If you are getting into SA hit up Tj!! Like seriously DO IT!!!

Leah Epstein
Would I recommend training with Tj?
For me to give 5*'s...you have got to earn them, I don't give them out easily.

Did Tj earn himself 5*'s?

ABSOLUTELY, without a doubt or hesitation!
You might find Tj's training different from the norm'.
This is because he 'is bothered', he takes time and cares about whether you 'get it' or not and doesn't give up until you 'DO' get it!
This deserves a whole heap of respect in my book!
Tj is so thorough with his teaching that I would go so far as to say, "If you are not successful following the training and support Tj supplies you with, point your finger in the mirror, not at Tj!
Great, fun training... HIGHLY recommend this guy

<u>Aliyah Oye</u>

I attended TJ's serviced accommodation training 19th October 2019. I was amazed at how well TJ was able to explain fairly complex information in a way that was easy to follow and understand. TJ was willing to continually go over concepts until everyone understood and took everyone's situations into consideration. TJ was friendly and approachable and was focused on ensuring that everyone took away as much information as possible feeling fully equipped to be able to implement these things in the real world. I am so impressed and would recommend to anyone that is planning to go into serviced accommodation. There was no
up selling or feeling pressured to part with more money. You get exactly what you paid for. Thanks a lot TJ and the team.

Pelegia Amai

I did Tj's online training which I still refer to if I get confused. The good thing is he keeps on updating the online course and I don't have to pay to use the updated tutorials. Just one payment is enough. The other good thing is you can listen to his tutorials a dozen and a half times if you didn't get it the first time for no extra change Thank you Tj Atkinson I am running my SA in Southampton. And I'm happy very happy.

Rochael Stephenson

Tj is an amazing mentor and trainer. After meeting and working with him I've been able to make an ROI in less than 2 months! If your looking for an SA and deal sourcing trainer Tj is your guy. He is honest and truly wants his students to succeed!

Epi Mabika

I did some SA training with Tj and found him to be a highly knowledgeable and seasoned professional. He didn't fluff around like some do, but delivered content with clarity & precision, keeping us engaged throughout.

This was an intensive training, however there was no overwhelm or confusion afterwards. Instead, I left with clear strategies and confidence to go out there and start winning.

He exceeded my expectations and patiently answered every question, leaving no stone unturned.

If you want results in your business, Tj is the person to hire. I highly recommend & endorse any of his trainings or services. The post training support is also great as Tj does all he can to ensure your success.

He is one of the best in the industry and this is one of the best investments I've made this year. Thank you Tj!

Joan MK

I just completed day two of SA & Deal packaging training. The most rewarding two days. I learnt so much from someone with great knowledge and experience. TJ is very humble and you can tell right from the beginning that his goal is to see you win. He goes through everything step by step, answers every single question and actually encourages you to ask questions as you go along.

If you want someone who will not sugar coat anything and will openly tell you what to expect while teaching you how to win but also how to deal with the obstacles, then TJ is the man.

Thank you TJ for serving me with your gift, you have boosted my confidence in taking the first steps towards SA & Deal packaging. I left very motivated. Ready to become a SA beast!

Sabha Anwar

I have one word for TJ's training... WOW! As a recent graduate, I know the importance of not only teaching but engaging students and TJ did just that. It was a long day ahead of us, minus the protests - but TJ made the SA training enjoyable and I was engaged the entire day from start to finish. He shared amazing tips and useful information to make the process for SA easier! I have learned so much and can't wait to begin my property venture! I will definitely be attending the sourcing course very soon. Amazing teacher, comedic and very easy to talk too. Very rare to find someone like this! Thank you so much and I really mean everything in this review. Wow! Definitely worth investing in his course!!!

Maku Obuobi

The training with TJ on SA was really useful and insightful. The training is informed by years of experience working through guidelines, dealing with booking platforms and guests - and so very practical and comprehensive.

Afua Serwaa

When I booked to spend one whole day with Tj I wondered why we needed all that time. I found he has such an in-depth knowledge of SA, the whole day wasn't enough! And I was glad I hadn't got my first unit as I could have made a lot of mistakes. His practical knowledge gives him clout to teach the subject.

Please don't get started in SA without any training. And if you are looking for a trainer, I wholeheartedly recommend Tj.

Khadija Owusu

Tj's SA course was amazing! He took the time to not only thoroughly explain the process but also honestly explained the highs and lows. Some of which he has personally experienced. Overall this was a fantastic day filled with a lot of knowledge and meeting new people. I'm happy I attended the course!

Onome Onuma

I attended TJ's training last week. It was fantastic. TJ is a rare combination of a professional property guru that is full of expertise as well as engaging. He is extremely knowledgable in his craft with excellent communication skills and the delivery of his training to students is superlative. He offers a solution for every eventuality and is very patient and very open. So NO question is too silly.

I would recommend him with all confidence. His training would be an invaluable asset at any stage in the property industry, be it beginner, intermediate or pro. I simply cannot endorse TJ and his training enough. If you are considering, please go for it knowing it will absolutely be a worthwhile investment.

Funke Adedoyin

The training was everything promised and many more. TJ went in-depth into how to start the business and pitfalls to watch out for. Definitely got much more than the money's worth.

A heartfelt thank you to you TJ.

Ezugo Okoma

Honestly, I've been to a few property trainings both free and paid. And I can definitely say that this has been one of the few trainings that has been so valuable!

If you read any of the reviews on TJ's training one of the things you'll hear is that he is honest and he doesn't hide anything and this is so true.

We were able to get our first deal within 30 days of having training with TJ and experienced the some issues he had taught on previously and knew precisely how to deal with it.

I couldn't recommend him enough!

Morenike Okoma

I would definitely recommend this course! TJ wasn't only excellent in teaching but honest about both the highs and lows in Serviced Accommodation. And because of this I was able to manage my expectations.

I was a beginner when I attended this course and only had basic knowledge of SA but after his course was able to acquire my first unit with my husband within 30 days!

During the course TJ is an open book and is incredibly patient. I would recommend for both beginners and those that are already within the business!

Would you like to learn how to start your own Serviced Accommodation Property Business?
Contact me at www.tjatkinson.com immediately to sign up to our training program.

Glossary

REVPAR

ADR (or ARR) – Average Daily Rate, or Average Room Rate (calculated by dividing revenue generated from income from hotel rooms sold by the total number of rooms sold

Advance Offers – Generally discounted rates to encourage guests to book in advance.

BAR – Best Available Rates (typically rates that are the 'best available' at the time of booking, often these are short lead bookings)

Channel Management – The process a hotel uses to update ARI (Availability, Rates and Inventory) in various distribution channels.

ETA – Estimated Time of Arrival.

IBE – Internet Booking Engine.

LOS (or Length of Stay) – The duration of a guests visit. E.g 3 nights.

MLOS – Minimum Length of Stay.

Net Rate – A wholesale rate to allow a third party markup.

NS (or No Show) – A guest who doesn't show up, despite having a reservation.

Occ (or Occupancy) – The rate of occupation of a hotels total rooms, at any given time. For example, an occupancy rate of 95% would mean that 95% of a hotels room inventory is presently occupied.

OTA – Online Travel Agent/Agency. A 3rd party who often sells a hotels room inventory on their behalf (and is paid a commission for any bookings referred) Examples of some of the main OTA's include Expedia, Booking.com, Hotels.com etc.

Parity – The policy of providing consistency between all sales channels. Commonly associated with rate parity, but can include room type, content parity etc.

Pax – Number of people/passengers. E.g) 6 pax would be 6 people/passengers.

Rack Rate – The standard or default rate for a room, before any discounts (for example, advance purchase discounts) are applied.

Yield Management – The practice of raising or lowering prices based on demand.

Would you like to learn how to start your own Serviced Accommodation Property Business?
Contact me at www.tjatkinson.com immediately to sign up to our training program.

Printed in Poland
by Amazon Fulfillment
Poland Sp. z o.o., Wrocław

55185556R00089